Pebble®
Plus

Science and Engineering Practices

FINDING INFORMATION
AND MAKING ARGUMENTS

by Riley Flynn

CAPSTONE PRESS
a capstone imprint

Pebble Plus is published by Capstone Press,
1710 Roe Crest Drive, North Mankato, Minnesota 56003
www.mycapstone.com

Library of Congress Cataloging-in-Publication Data
Cataloging-in-Publication data is on file with the Library of Congress.
ISBN 978-1-5157-0948-0 (library binding)
ISBN 978-1-5157-0980-0 (paperback)
ISBN 978-1-5157-1115-5 (eBook PDF)

Editorial Credits
Anna Butzer, editor; Sarah Bennett, designer; Eric Gohl, media researcher; Laura Manthe, production specialist

Photo Credits
Capstone: 9, 11; Shutterstock: Becky Sheridan, 17, Ivan Kuzmin, 19, Kdonmuang, 7, kozzi, 20, Monkey Business
Images, 13, overcrew, 15, PointImages, 5, wavebreakmedia, cover

Design Elements: Shutterstock

Note to Parents and Teachers

The Science and Engineering Practices set supports Next Generation Science Standards
related to Science and Engineering Practices. This book describes and illustrates finding
information and making arguments. The images support early readers in understanding the
text. The repetition of words and phrases helps early readers learn new words. This book
also introduces early readers to subject-specific vocabulary words, which are defined in the
Glossary section. Early readers may need assistance to read some words and to use the
Table of Contents, Glossary, Read More, Internet Sites, Critical Thinking Using the Common
Core, and Index sections of the book.

Printed and bound in China.
007714

Table of Contents

Think Like a Scientist 4

Use Text Features 8

Facts and Evidence 12

Activity: Finding Information
and Making Claims 20

Glossary 22

Read More 23

Internet Sites 23

Critical Thinking
Using the Common Core 24

Index 24

Think Like a Scientist

Scientists look for information to understand our world. Information helps them test ideas and solve problems. To think like a scientist, you need to look for information too.

Where can you find information?
You can read a book or
an online article. You can also
watch a video about a topic.
Information is all around us.

Use Text Features

Text features can help you find

key information when you read.

Start with the table of contents.

Then look for headings,

bold print, and sidebars.

World o

The **dinosau**
that lived mi
dinosaurs w
that ever wa
was 75 feet l
as a bus. The
was 36 feet l
long as a cc

Saurophagana

12 *Apatosa*

a group of animals
years ago. Some
biggest animals
Earth. *Apatosaurus*
out twice as long
Saurophaganax
ore than twice as

Did You Know?

Torosaurus had the largest head of any land animal. It was 8 feet long. That's longer than an average bed!

Torosaurus

13

9

Pictures also hold information.
You are reading about dinosaurs.
What do the different dinosaurs
look like? Do the pictures have
labels? These features help you
understand the text.

One of the lo
sauropod co
to be 89 feet
than the leng
Sauropods liv
animals walk
they could b
older dinosau

14   *Diplodo*

k

inosaurs was a
lodocus. It grew
at is longer
swimming pool.
erds. The younger
center where
ted by the larger,

Saltasaurus

15

Facts and Evidence

Gathering information helps you build arguments. To argue about a topic you need to know facts. We can prove a fact to be true. We can't prove an opinion.

Arguments need facts. You say that we should not throw trash in a lake. Why? A fish might think trash is food. Trash can hurt the fish. That is a fact.

Every argument also has two parts. The first part is a claim. The claim is the main point. You can claim that some animals see well in the dark.

The second part of an argument is evidence. You have observed bats flying and eating in the dark. That's strong evidence to prove your claim.

Finding Information and Making Claims

Which food attracts the most insects at a picnic? Find out!

What You Need

- pencil
- paper
- honey or sugar
- bread
- hot dog, cut up into small pieces
- 3 jar lids
- ruler
- timer, clock, or watch

What You Do

1. Draw three columns on the piece of paper. Write a food item in each column.

2. Place a small amount of each food on a jar lid. Set the lids outside. Place the lids about 3 inches (7.6 centimeters) from each other.

3. Observe the lids. Write down the time you start watching the lids.

4. Each time an insect inspects a food, place a check mark under its column. Also list the type of insect.

5. How long did it take for each food to attract its first insect? Add this information to each column.

What Do You Think?

Make a claim. A claim is something you believe to be true. Which type of food attracts the most insects at a picnic? Why? Now share what you learned with a friend.

Glossary

argument—a disagreement between two or more people

claim—to say that something is true help prove something to be true or false

evidence—information, items, and facts that help prove something to be true or false

fact—information that is truthful and correct

gather—to collect things

label—a descriptive or identifying word or phrase

observe—to watch someone or something closely in order to learn something

opinion—a person's ideas and beliefs about something

problem—something that causes trouble

Read More

Rustad, Martha E.H. *Learning About Fact and Opinion.* Media Literacy for Kids. North Mankato, Minn.: Capstone Press, 2015.

Yearling, Tricia. *How Do I Find Information Online?* Online Smarts. New York: Enslow Publishing, 2016.

Internet Sites

FactHound offers a safe, fun way to find Internet sites related to this book. All of the sites on FactHound have been researched by our staff.

Here's all you do:
Visit www.facthound.com
Type in this code: 9781515709480

 Check out projects, games and lots more at
www.capstonekids.com

Critical Thinking Using the Common Core

1. What is a fact? (Key Ideas and Details)

2. Look at the pictures on pages 9 and 11. What text features do you see? (Integration of Knowledge and Ideas)

Index

articles, 6

books, 6

claim, 16, 18

evidence, 18

facts, 12, 14

ideas, 4

observations, 18

opinions, 12

problems, 4

scientists, 4

solutions, 4

text features, 8, 10

videos, 6